THE WILL KIT

Create your own legally effective will

Disclaimer

The information contained in *The Will Kit* is intended as a guide to the law relating to the making of a valid Will in Australia and should not be used as a substitute for legal advice. We make no warranties or representations about the content. We attempt to ensure that the content is current but we do not guarantee its currency. We are not responsible to you or anyone else for any indirect, incidental, special or consequential loss suffered in connection with the use of any of the content. If you are uncertain about your Will or your situation is complex or complicated, the advice of a legally qualified person should be sought.

First published in 2004 by New Holland Publishers
London • Sydney • Auckland

131–151 Great Titchfield Street, London WIW 5BB, United Kingdom
1/66 Gibbes Street, Chatswood, NSW 2067, Australia
5/39 Woodside Ave, Northcote, Auckland 0627, New Zealand

newhollandpublishers.com

A record of this book is held at the British Library and the National Library of Australia.

ISBN 9781760790448

Group Managing Director: Fiona Schultz
Printed in China by Toppan Leefung Printing Ltd.

10 9 8 7 6 5 4 3 2 1

Keep up with New Holland Publishers on Facebook
facebook.com/NewHollandPublishers

CONTENTS

1. GLOSSARY

Beneficiary: A person who receives all or part of a deceased person's Estate.

Bequest: A gift of personal item/s.

Codicil: A codicil is a document, separate to the original Will, which sets out alterations or additions to the Will. The codicil must be signed by the Willmaker in the same way that a Will is and must specifically refer to the original Will.

Devise: A devise is a gift of land (this includes all buildings and anything else permanently attached to the land).

Estate: The assets of a deceased person.

Executor/Executors: The person/s nominated in a Will to carry out the terms of the Will and deal with the Estate. An Executor must be over the age of eighteen.

Intestate: Dying without leaving a Will or dying with only parts of the Will being valid. In these circumstances, the deceased's Estate will be distributed in accordance with a schedule stipulated by legislation.

Intestacy Rules: The rules that apply in the absence of a Will (or a complete Will) which determine distribution of the Estate of a person who dies intestate.

Joint Tenancy: Property owned by two or more people equally. Upon death of one of those people, the property passes automatically to the other co-owner(s) no matter what the deceased's Will says.

Legacy: A gift of money to a certain person, group of people or organisation.

Power of Attorney: A legal document which gives one or more people the power to act on behalf of another in financial or legal matters. A power of attorney is not a Will. It operates whilst the person who makes it (the grantor/donor) is still alive and lapses upon the death of that person or when revoked by the grantor/donor during their lifetime.

Probate: Probate is certification by a court that the Will is valid and permits the Executor to commence distribution of the Estate in accordance with the terms of the Will. If the Willmaker holds assets in multiple states in Australia a grant of probate will need to be resealed in each state. If the Willmaker holds assets overseas it is advisable for separate wills to be created according to the laws of each country.

Residuary: Is the remainder of an Estate after bequests, legacies and devises have been given.

Tenancy in Common: Where property is owned by one or more person and each has a separate share (as distinct from a joint tenancy). The share passes to beneficiaries under a Will or the intestacy rules, and not to surviving co-owners.

Testamentary Guardian: A person or persons nominated in the Will as guardian for children (minors) of the Willmaker. A guardian has responsibility for the day to day management and care of the child. It should be noted that a surviving parent will generally assume guardianship. The Willmaker should consult first with any person that they intend to nominate as a guardian.

Testate: Dying and leaving a valid Will.

Trustee: A trustee is a person who manages the assets of another person (usually children) for the benefit of those persons. After Probate of a Will is granted, an Executor becomes a trustee of any trusts established by that Will.

Willmaker: The person who has made a Will.

2. THE WILL KIT

(For assets held within Australia)

i. What is a Will?

A Will is a written document that sets out how a person (the Willmaker) wants their assets (Estate) dealt with after their death. It is a document that provides for an orderly and cost-effective means to distribute assets to those persons identified in the Will as recipients (beneficiaries). To be valid, a Will must include certain formal requirements, details of which are included in *The Will Kit*.

ii. What is *The Will Kit*?

The Will Kit is designed to provide basic information as a guide to drafting a legally enforceable Will. Set out at the back of *The Will Kit* are blank pro forma Wills to be used to create simple Wills that are legal everywhere in Australia. These blank Wills have been designed especially for:

- a single person
- a married person/person in a de facto relationship who has children, including a married person in a gay or lesbian relationship
- a married person/person in a de facto relationship who does not have children, including a married person in a gay or lesbian relationship

Only one copy of each type of Will is supplied in *The Will Kit*. It is recommended that you make a photocopy of the appropriate Will before filling out the Will to use as practice. Each Willmaker must complete a separate Will.

Although there is no requirement that a lawyer must draft a Will for it to be legally enforceable, and a person can write their own Will, it is strongly recommended that if your Will is complex you should use a lawyer or a trustee company to draft your Will.

iii. Dying without a Will

Dying without a Will is referred to as dying intestate. If a person dies intestate all assets that they own outright will be disposed of strictly in accordance with a schedule of persons stipulated by legislation (the intestacy rules). These persons include the deceased's closest relatives (including de factos) but in circumstances where no relatives can be established, the Estate will pass to the Crown. Importantly, gay and lesbian relationships are included in the intestacy rules.

iv. Who can make a Will?

Any person who is over eighteen years of age can make a Will. Wills can also be made by persons younger than eighteen years of age if they are or have been married, the court has granted leave to the minor to make a Will, or the Will is made in contemplation of a marriage which subsequently occurs. If the Will is made in contemplation of marriage the proposed spouse's name and the anticipated marriage date should be incorporated into the Will. It is important that the Willmaker be mentally capable of knowing that they are making a Will.

v. Who should make a Will

As a general principle, everyone who is over the age of eighteen years should make a Will regardless of their status and/or asset situation. In addition, there are certain categories of people who **must** make a Will, as dying without a Will could seriously jeopardise their expectations about what would happen to their assets on their death. These groups include:

(a) Persons with substantial assets:
Anyone who owns, in their own name, a house and/or land (as distinct from married couples who jointly own a home). This can include someone who is married and who owns an investment property.

(b) Persons in gay and lesbian relationships:
The law now treats gay and lesbian couples the same way it treats married or heterosexual couples in de facto relationships.

(c) Extended families:
A person who has divorced and has remarried or entered a de facto relationship should make a Will as their Estate may be complicated by claims arising from:

- their own children
- their partner (whether married or de facto)
- children of their partner (from their partner's former relationships)

People who fall within the above categories should seek legal advice in the preparation of their Wills.

vi. When should you change your Will?

You should change your Will:

- When you marry, remarry or divorce. Marriage revokes Wills made prior to the marriage (unless the Will was made in contemplation of marriage). Accordingly, any person who has recently been married should make a Will. Divorce will not revoke the whole Will but it will revoke any gift to a former spouse and the appointment of that spouse as Executor, Trustee or Guardian will be omitted from the Will.
- If you change your mind about who will get what share of your Estate.
- If one (or more) of the beneficiaries named or nominated in your Will dies.

3. FORMAL REQUIREMENTS FOR A VALID WILL

i. Formal requirements

In order to be valid a Will must:

- be in writing (typed or handwritten)
- on its face, give the appearance of being a Will
- be signed by the Willmaker in the presence of two adult witnesses who must be present at the same time
- be signed by the two adult witnesses in the presence of the Willmaker
- **the adult witnesses must not be beneficiaries or the spouse/partner of the Willmaker**

ii. Steps to follow when signing the Will

To ensure that the Will meets the formal requirements, the following steps should be adhered to.

1. The Willmaker must read, understand and be happy with the entire Will.
2. Two adult witnesses **must** be present.
3. The Willmaker and the two adult witnesses should all use the same pen.
4. The Will should be dated before it is signed.
5. In the presence of the two witnesses, the Willmaker should sign at the bottom of each page and at the attestation clause on the last page of the Will.
6. In the presence of the Willmaker and each other, the witnesses should sign the Will at the bottom of each page and at the attestation clause on the last page of the Will. The witnesses should also print their name and address below their signature at the attestation clause.
7. At the time of signing, any alterations or amendments to the Will **must** be initialled by the Willmaker and the two adult witnesses.
8. After signing, **no** amendments or alterations should be made to the Will.
9. There should be only one original Will. Copies can be made and endorsed with the word 'copy'.

4. DRAFTING THE WILL

i. Preparation

Before you actually start to prepare your Will, you will need to write down a certain amount of personal information. This makes it easier to write your Will and can assist your Executor in doing their job.

Before writing the Will, the Willmaker should:

- **List all of his or her ASSETS.** This may include real estate or other large assets such as furniture, jewellery or motor vehicles and the like. You do not need to list every item but you may wish to leave specific items to individual beneficiaries. If at the time of your death, a specific listed item no longer exists, your Will remains valid but the specified gift will fail. Make a list of your investments if you would like to leave them to a Beneficiary. Superannuation and insurance policies usually have a nominated Beneficiary within them, but writing them down completes the task of listing your assets.

- **List all of his or her DEBTS and LIABILITIES.** Your liabilities do not need to be listed in your Will, however it is a good idea to write these down and keep them as separate notes with a copy of the Will. Your liabilities could include mortgages or other secured loans on real estate, bank or other institutional loans, credit card liabilities, and any money owed to private individuals or to the Australian Taxation Office.

- **List the BENEFICIARIES.** The accurate identification of Beneficiaries is important as they may need to be identified many years into the future. These details may include their full names, address, date of birth and their relationship to you. If at the time of your death an individual Beneficiary to whom a specific item has been bequeathed is no longer alive,your will should either identify an alternate Beneficiary or specifically state that the specific item in this situation will form part of the Residuary. If you appoint a charity or organisation as a Beneficiary it is essential that the correct name of the institution is incorporated into the Will. If at the time of your death the charity or organisation no longer exists your will should either list an alternate charity or organisation, grant the Executor the power to appoint an alternate charity or organisation that fulfills the same objects or state that the gift is to form part of the Residuary. If the Willmaker identifies 'my children' as beneficiaries under the will, the term 'my children' will also include children of previous relationships, adopted children and ex nuptial children unless the children are specifically named or the Will states otherwise.

- **Select the EXECUTOR/S.** This can be one or more persons but whoever is chosen must be over the age of eighteen years. Make sure before listing the Executor/s that they are willing to take on the responsibility. Keep in mind that you may want to select person/s who are not likely to predecease you. Unlike the situation with witnesses, your Executor can be a Beneficiary in your Will.

- **Select a person to be TESTAMENTARY GUARDIAN.** If you presently have minor children (under the age of eighteen years) then you may need to decide who you would like to appoint to be their legal guardian/s. It will be helpful to list as many details as you can about the guardian/s. Make sure before listing the guardian/s that they are willing to take on the responsibility of this role. In the pro forma Will for a married person who has children a clause for guardianship of minor children has been inserted at clause 5.

Use the tables provided on the following pages to help you in your preparation. It is recommended that you use a photocopy of the appropriate Will to practise before starting to fill in your Will. A Sample Will and explanatory notes have been provided on pages 12–15 to assist you in completing a Will.

List of assets

	Solely held	Jointly held	Approx. Value
Real Estate			
Address:			
Money on Account at Bank/Building Society			
Institution: Account No.			
Shares			
Institution: No. of Shares held			
Vehicles			
Make Registration No.			
Other			

List of liabilities

Property or item	Lender	Loan or Mortgage Number	Original Amount	Start Date	Paid Out Date	Other

List of possible executors

Name of Executor	Address	Relationship

List of possible beneficiaries

Relationship	Name	Asset 1	Asset 2	Others
Spouse/Partner				
First Child				
Second Child				
Grandchildren				
Friends				
Relatives				
Charity or Organisation				

ii. Sample Will

THIS IS THE LAST WILL AND TESTAMENT of me[1] *James Bellamy*
of 15 Astridge Street, Ryde, NSW 1680, plumber

1. I REVOKE all former wills and testamentary dispositions made by me AND DECLARE this to be my last Will and Testament.[2]

2. I APPOINT *Frank Smith*[3] of *1 Cedar Grove Batemans Bay NSW 2536* and *Jane Smith* of *74 Tennyson Street Elwood VIC 3184* to be the joint Executors and Trustees of this my Will (referred to herein as 'my Trustees') PROVIDED HOWEVER that if either one or both dies before me or is unwilling or unable through sickness or accident to act as my Executor and Trustee THEN I APPOINT *Howard Jones* of *10 Lake Street, Ballina NSW 2478* as my substitute Executor and Trustee.

3. I MAKE the following bequests free of all costs:-[4]

   a. I GIVE *my car at the date of my death* to *John Jones*

   b. I GIVE my *watch* to *Peter Smith*

   ~~c. I GIVE my .... to ....~~

   ~~d. I GIVE my .... to ....~~

Willmaker	Witness	Witness
Jaes Bellamy	Marie Stopes	Shaun Keane

1. Identification: Complete the full name, address and occupation of the Willmaker.

2. Revocation: This revokes earlier Wills and Codicils.

3. Executor Appointment: In this clause the Willmaker needs to identify the person/s who will carry out the instructions conferred in the Will. It is wise to nominate more than one Executor, in case the person you nominate dies or refuses to act. The Willmaker should check with the Executor(s) that they are willing to act in this capacity.

4. Special Bequests: The Willmaker sets out specific items to be left to particular people as gifts. The items should be clearly described to avoid confusion. This type of clause is well suited for gifts of personal possessions, such as jewellery and furniture. If you use the pro forma Will attached in *The Will Kit*, please ensure you cross out any blank space not utilised (as can be seen above).

4. I GIVE DEVISE AND BEQUEATH the residue of my real and personal property of whatever nature and kind and wherever it is located or to which I shall be seised possessed or entitled at my death or over which I shall then have a general power of appointment (called 'my Estate') UNTO my Trustees upon the following trusts:[5]

   (a) UPON TRUST that my Trustees shall sell, call in collect and convert into money my Estate at such time or times and in such manner as my Trustees think fit with power to postpone the sale, calling in or conversion, or the sale of any part or parts of my Estate during such period as my Trustees think proper and to retain the same or any part thereof in its present form without being responsible for loss;

   (b) UPON TRUST to pay all my debts funeral and testamentary expenses including all duties and taxes payable in respect of my Estate or in consequence of my death;

   (c) UPON TRUST to give as follows:

   i. to *Ross Brown* .... the sum of *ten thousand dollars* .... (\$*10,000.00*)
   ii. to *The Salvation Army* .... the sum of *five thousand dollars*.......................... (\$*5,000.00*)
   iii. to *St Vincent de Paul* .... the sum of *five thousand dollars*.......................... (\$*5,000.00*)
   ~~iv. to .... the sum of \$..................................~~

   PROVIDED THAT

   (1) if any of the bequests numbered (i–iii) fail for any reason whatsoever such bequest(s) shall form part of the Residuary.
   (2) if any of the beneficiaries numbered (ii) and (iii) cease to exist then my Executor shall pay it to a charitable organisation which they consider most nearly fulfills the objects I intend to benefit, and if none then such bequest is to form part of my Residuary.

   (d) the balance of the residue of my Estate UPON TRUST for *Peter Smith*, of 7 *Elizabeth Bay Road, Elizabeth Bay NSW 2011*
   PROVIDED HOWEVER that if she/he should predecease me leaving a child or children living at my death such child or children shall take and if more than one as tenants in common in equal shares the share which their said parent would have taken if he or she survived me.

Willmaker	Witness	Witness
....	....	....

5. Residual Estate: This clause deals with the balance of the Willmaker's property which is not bequeathed by specific gift. It is **vital** that this section be completed, otherwise any assets not dealt with as specific gifts will be intestate and distributed according to the intestacy rules. The residual Estate also deals with assets acquired after the Will is made. It should be noted that the Executor/Trustee will be empowered to call in and convert the residual Estate to cash so that specific gifts of cash can be made out of the residual Estate. If you use the pro forma Will attached in *The Will Kit*, please ensure you cross out any blank space not utilised (as can be seen above).

5. I DECLARE that my Trustees will have the following powers[6] (exercisable in the absolute discretion of my Trustees) in addition to those conferred on executors and trustees by statute:-

   (a) to retain without being liable for any loss (including liability for taxation on capital gain) caused by so doing, any asset investment or security held by me at my death and to invest any moneys available for investment in any investment of whatever nature and kind whether trustee investments or otherwise;

   (b) to sell, mortgage, lease, exchange or otherwise dispose of the whole or such part or parts of my Estate as my Trustees may consider necessary or expedient, such power to be exercised as though my Trustees were the absolute beneficial owner of my Estate;

   (c) to apply the whole or any part or parts of the income or capital of the expectant presumptive contingent or vested share of any beneficiary under this my Will for or towards his or her maintenance education benefit or advancement with power to pay the same to the guardian of or person with whom any minor beneficiary shall be residing without being responsible to see to the application of that benefit;

   (d) to appropriate and partition any real or personal property forming part of my Estate (and for such purposes to determine the values thereof) to or towards the share of any beneficiary or beneficiaries under my Will without obtaining any of the consents made necessary by statute;

Willmaker	Witness	Witness
....	....	....

6. Trustee's Powers: Set out in paragraphs (a) to (g) are specific examples of trustees powers. Such powers are in addition to powers a trustee may exercise pursuant to legislation. The Willmaker can delete any of the nominated trustees' powers by crossing out the appropriate clause/s. The powers specified in paragraph (a) to (g) are designed to give the trustee maximum flexibility to look after assets for beneficiaries who are under eighteen years of age or assets which the Willmaker instructs to be kept in trust after death.

(e) to determine in all cases of doubt whether any money coming into the hands of my Trustees is capital or income or whether any loss or outgoings should be charged against capital or income;

(f) to exercise sell or refrain from exercising any right or privilege arising out of the ownership of any shares or other investment;

(g) to manage any part of any Estate and to carry on any business conducted by me at the date of my death (whether conducted alone or in partnership with any other person) with these powers to be exercised as though my Trustees were the absolute beneficial owners of my Estate.

DATED this .... [DAY] .... [MONTH] .... [YEAR]

SIGNED[7] by the Willmaker in our presence and attested by us in the presence of her/him and of each other.

Jaren Bellamy ....

Willmaker's signature

Witness 1	**Witness 2**
Signature: Marie Slopes	**Signature:** Shaun Keane
Name: Marie Slopes	**Name:** Shaun Keane
Address: 2/5 Bellevue St. Fairfield 2165	**Address:** 84 Raglan St. La Perouse 2036

7. Attestation of Will: This is where the Will is signed by the Willmaker in the presence of two adult witnesses, who also sign the Will. The Willmaker and the two adult witnesses must use the same pen and the witnesses must set out their names and addresses. Any changes must be dated and signed by all parties. The witnesses **must not** be beneficiaries of the Will or the spouse/partner of the Willmaker.

SAFEKEEPING OF YOUR WILL

The Will must be easily found after the Willmaker dies, otherwise a court can presume that the Will was destroyed and the Willmaker will die intestate.

It is vital to keep the original Will in a safe place, such as a safety deposit box at your bank or in safe custody with your lawyer or the public trustee. A copy of the Will should be kept at the Willmaker's home and it is advisable to provide a copy to the Executor/s. These copies should also indicate the location of the original Will.

NOTES

5. I DECLARE that my Trustees shall have the following powers (exercisable in the absolute discretion of my Trustees) in addition to those conferred on executors and trustees by statute:
   (a) to retain without being liable for any loss (including liability for taxation on capital gain) caused by so doing, any asset investment or security held by me at my death and to invest any moneys available for investment in any investment of whatever nature whether trustee investments or otherwise;
   (b) to sell, mortgage, lease, exchange or otherwise dispose of the whole or such part or parts of my Estate as my Trustees may consider necessary or expedient, such power to be exercised as though my Trustees were the absolute beneficial owner of my Estate;
   (c) to apply the whole or any parts of the income or capital of the expectant presumptive contingent or vested share of any beneficiary under this my Will for or towards his or her maintenance education benefit or advancement with power to pay the same to the guardian or person with whom any minor beneficiary shall be residing without being responsible to see the application thereof;
   (d) to appropriate and partition any real or personal property forming part of my Estate (and for such purposes to determine the values thereof) to or towards the share of any beneficiary or beneficiaries under my Will without obtaining any of the consents made necessary by statute;
   (e) to determine in all cases of doubt whether any money coming into the hands of my Trustees is capital or income or whether any loss or outgoings should be charged against capital or income;
   (f) to exercise sell or refrain from exercising any right or privilege arising out of the ownership of any shares or other investment;
   (g) to manage any part of any Estate and to carry on any business conducted by me at the date of my death (whether conducted alone or in partnership with any other person) with powers to be exercised as though my Trustees were the absolute beneficial owners of my Estate.

DATED this ....[DAY] ....[MONTH] .... [YEAR]

SIGNED by the Willmaker in our presence and attested by us in the presence of her/him and of each other.

....
Willmaker's signature

Witness 1	**Witness 2** ....
Signature:	**Signature:** ....
Name:	**Name:** ....
Address:	**Address:** ....

Will for a

SINGLE PERSON

THIS IS THE LAST WILL AND TESTAMENT OF

....

DATED: ....

THIS IS THE LAST WILL AND TESTAMENT of me ....[NAME]

of .... [ADDRESS] .... [OCCUPATION]

1. I REVOKE all former Wills and testamentary dispositions made by me AND DECLARE this to be my last Will and Testament.

2. I APPOINT .... of ....

   and .... of ....

   to be the joint Executors and Trustees of this my Will (referred to herein as 'my Trustees') PROVIDED HOWEVER that if either one or both dies before me or is unwilling or unable through sickness or accident to act as my Executor and Trustee THEN I APPOINT

   .... of ....

   as my substitute Executor and Trustee.

3. I MAKE the following bequests free of all costs:

   a. I GIVE my .... to ....
   b. I GIVE my .... to ....
   c. I GIVE my .... to ....
   d. I GIVE my .... to ....
   e. I GIVE my .... to ....
   f. I GIVE my .... to ....
   g. I GIVE my .... to ....
   h. I GIVE my .... to ....

   PROVIDED THAT if any of the above bequests fail for any reason whatsoever such bequest(s) shall form part of the Residuary.

Willmaker	Witness	Witness
....	....	....

4. I GIVE DEVISE AND BEQUEATH the residue of my real and personal property of whatever nature and kind and wherever it is located or to which I shall be seised possessed or entitled at my death or over which I shall then have a general power of appointment (called 'my Estate') UNTO my Trustees upon the following trusts:

(a) UPON TRUST that my Trustees shall sell, call in collect and convert into money my Estate at such time or times and in such manner as my Trustees think fit with power to postpone the sale, calling in or conversion, or the sale of any part or parts of my Estate during such period as my Trustees think proper and to retain the same or any part thereof in its present form without being responsible for loss;

(b) UPON TRUST to pay all my debts funeral and testamentary expenses including all duties and taxes payable in respect of my Estate or in consequence of my death;

(c) UPON TRUST to give as follows:

i. to .... the sum of .... ($ ....)

ii. to .... the sum of .... ($ ....)

iii. to .... the sum of .... ($ ....)

iv. to .... the sum of .... ($ ....)

v. to .... the sum of .... ($ ....)

PROVIDED THAT if any of the above bequests fail for any reason whatsoever such bequest(s) shall form part of the Residuary.

(d) the balance of the residue of my Estate UPON TRUST to .... [NAME] of .... [ADDRESS]

PROVIDED HOWEVER that if she/he should predecease me leaving a child or children living at my death such child or children shall take and if more than one as tenants in common in equal shares the share which their parent would have taken if he or she survived me.

Willmaker	Witness	Witness
....	....	....

4. I DECLARE that my Trustees will have the following powers (exercisable in the absolute discretion of my Trustees) in addition to those conferred on executors and trustees by statute:

   (a) to retain without being liable for any loss (including liability for taxation on capital gain) caused by so doing, any asset investment or security held by me at my death, and to invest any moneys available for investment in any investment of whatever nature and kind whether trustee investments or otherwise;

   (b) to sell, mortgage, lease, exchange or otherwise dispose of the whole or such part or parts of my Estate as my Trustees may consider necessary or expedient, such power to be exercised as though my Trustees were the absolute beneficial owner of my Estate;

   (c) to apply the whole or any part or parts of the income or capital of the expectant presumptive contingent or vested share of any beneficiary under this my Will for or towards his or her maintenance education benefit or advancement with power to pay the same to the guardian of or person with whom any minor beneficiary shall be residing without being responsible to see to the application thereof;

   (d) to appropriate and partition any real or personal property forming part of my Estate (and for such purposes to determine the values thereof) to or towards the share of any beneficiary or beneficiaries under my Will without obtaining any of the consents made necessary by statute;

   (e) to determine in all cases of doubt whether any money coming into the hands of my Trustees is capital or income or whether any loss or outgoings should be charged against capital or income;

   (f) to exercise sell or refrain from exercising any right or privilege arising out of the ownership of any shares or other investment;

   (g) to manage any part of any Estate and to carry on any business conducted by me at the date of my death (whether conducted alone or in partnership with any other person) with these powers to be exercised as though my Trustees were the absolute beneficial owners of my Estate.

Willmaker	Witness	Witness
....	....	....

THIS IS THE LAST WILL AND TESTAMENT of me ....[NAME]

of .... [ADDRESS] .... [OCCUPATION]

1. I REVOKE all former wills and testamentary dispositions made by me AND DECLARE this to be my last Will and Testament.

2. I APPOINT my WIFE/HUSBAND [STRIKE OUT WHICHEVER DOES NOT APPLY] ....[NAME] the sole Executor of this Will but if she/he predeceases me or is unable or unwilling to act in that capacity THEN I APPOINT

   ....[NAME] of ....[ADDRESS]

   ....[NAME] of ....[ADDRESS]

   to be the joint Executors and Trustees of this my Will (referred to as 'my Trustees').

3. I GIVE DEVISE AND BEQUEATH the whole of my Estate both real and personal of whatever nature and kind, wherever it is located (called 'my Estate') unto my wife/husband absolutely provided that she/he survives me by thirty days.

   (a) IF my wife/husband dies prior to attaining a vested interest in my Estate then I GIVE DEVISE AND BEQUEATH the whole of my Estate to my Trustees upon trust for all of my children including any adopted children, ex nuptial children and children from any other relationship/the children of my marriage to .... [NAME] [STRIKE OUT WHICHEVER DOES NOT APPLY] who survive me by thirty days and attain the age of .... years, and if more than one, in equal shares as tenants in common.

   (b) IF any such child of mine dies prior to attaining a vested interest in my Estate leaving a child or children at their death then such child or children will on attaining the age of .... years take equally the share which their parent would otherwise have taken under this my Will, and if more than one, in equal shares as tenants in common.

   (c) IF any such child of mine dies prior to attaining a vested interest in my Estate without leaving a child or children THEN I DIRECT that the share which that child would otherwise have taken be divided among all of my remaining children referred to in (a) above in equal shares as tenants in common.

Willmaker	Witness	Witness
....	....	....

Will for a

MARRIED PERSON WHO HAS CHILDREN

THIS IS THE LAST WILL AND TESTAMENT OF

....

DATED: ....

5. IF my wife/husband dies before me I APPOINT ....

and ....

or the survivor of them, as the testamentary guardians of my minor children.

DATED this ....[DAY] ....[MONTH]........................... [YEAR]

SIGNED by the Willmaker in our presence and attested by us in the presence of her/him and of each other.

....

Willmaker's signature

Witness 1	**Witness 2** ....
Signature:	**Signature:** ....
Name:	**Name:** ....
Address:	**Address:** ....

4. I GIVE DEVISE AND BEQUEATH the whole of my Estate both real and personal of whatever nature and kind, wherever it is located (called 'my Estate') UNTO my Trustees upon the following trusts:

(a) UPON TRUST that my Trustees shall sell, call in collect and convert into money my said Estate at such time or times and in such manner as my Trustees shall think fit with power to postpone the said sale calling in or conversion or the sale of any part or parts of my said Estate during such period as my Trustees shall think proper and to retain the same or any part thereof in its present form without being responsible for loss;

(b) UPON TRUST to pay all my debts funeral and testamentary expenses including all duties and taxes payable in respect of my Estate or in consequence of my death;

(c) UPON TRUST to give as follows:

i. to .... the sum of .... ($ ....)

ii. to .... the sum of .... ($ ....)

iii to .... the sum of .... ($ ....)

iv. to .... the sum of .... ($ ....)

v. to .... the sum of .... ($ ....)

PROVIDED THAT if any of the above bequests fail for any reason whatsoever such bequest(s) shall form part of the Residuary.

(d) the balance of the residue of my Estate UPON TRUST to ....[NAME]

of ....[ADDRESS]

PROVIDED HOWEVER that if she/he should predecease me leaving a child or children living at my death such child or children shall take and if more than one as tenants in common in equal shares the share which their parent would have taken if he or she survived me.

Willmaker	Witness	Witness
....	....	....

THIS IS THE LAST WILL AND TESTAMENT of me ....[NAME]

of .... [ADDRESS] .... [OCCUPATION]

1. I REVOKE all former wills and testamentary dispositions made by me AND DECLARE this to be my last Will and Testament.

2. I APPOINT my WIFE/HUSBAND [STRIKE OUT WHICHEVER DOES NOT APPLY]

   ....[NAME] the sole Executor of this Will but if

   she/he predeceases me or is unable or unwilling to act in that capacity THEN I APPOINT

   ....[NAME] of ....[ADDRESS]

   ....[NAME] of ....[ADDRESS]

   to be the joint Executors and Trustees of this my Will (referred to as 'my Trustees').

   I GIVE DEVISE AND BEQUEATH the whole of my Estate both real and personal of whatever nature and kind, wherever it is located (called 'my Estate') UNTO my wife/husband absolutely provided that she/he survives me by thirty days.

   (a) IF my wife/husband dies prior to attaining a vested interest in my Estate then the following provisions of my Will apply.

3. I MAKE the following bequests free of all costs:

   a. I GIVE my .... to ....
   b. I GIVE my .... to ....
   c. I GIVE my .... to ....
   d. I GIVE my .... to ....
   e. I GIVE my .... to ....
   f. I GIVE my .... to ....
   g. I GIVE my .... to ....
   h. I GIVE my .... to ....

   PROVIDED THAT if any of the above bequests fail for any reason whatsoever such bequest(s) shall form part of the Residuary.

Willmaker	Witness	Witness
....	....	....

Will for a

MARRIED PERSON WHO DOES NOT HAVE CHILDREN

THIS IS THE LAST WILL AND TESTAMENT OF

....

DATED: ....

5. I DECLARE that my Trustees shall have the following powers (exercisable in the absolute discretion of my Trustees) in addition to those conferred on executors and trustees by statute:
   (a) to retain without being liable for any loss (including liability for taxation on capital gain) caused by so doing, any asset investment or security held by me at my death and to invest any moneys available for investment in any investment of whatever nature whether trustee investments or otherwise;
   (b) to sell, mortgage, lease, exchange or otherwise dispose of the whole or such part or parts of my Estate as my Trustees may consider necessary or expedient, such power to be exercised as though my Trustees were the absolute beneficial owner of my Estate;
   (c) to apply the whole or any parts of the income or capital of the expectant presumptive contingent or vested share of any beneficiary under this my Will for or towards his or her maintenance education benefit or advancement with power to pay the same to the guardian or person with whom any minor beneficiary shall be residing without being responsible to see the application thereof;
   (d) to appropriate and partition any real or personal property forming part of my Estate (and for such purposes to determine the values thereof) to or towards the share of any beneficiary or beneficiaries under my Will without obtaining any of the consents made necessary by statute;
   (e) to determine in all cases of doubt whether any money coming into the hands of my Trustees is capital or income or whether any loss or outgoings should be charged against capital or income;
   (f) to exercise sell or refrain from exercising any right or privilege arising out of the ownership of any shares or other investment;
   (g) to manage any part of any Estate and to carry on any business conducted by me at the date of my death (whether conducted alone or in partnership with any other person) with powers to be exercised as though my Trustees were the absolute beneficial owners of my Estate.

DATED this ....[DAY] ....[MONTH] .... [YEAR]

SIGNED by the Willmaker in our presence and attested by us in the presence of her/him and of each other.

....

Willmaker's signature

Witness 1	**Witness 2** ....
Signature:	**Signature:** ....
Name:	**Name:** ....
Address:	**Address:** ....